# AFRICANIZING VEGAN FOOD

*ALL YOUR FAVOURITE NIGERIAN FOODS VEGANIZED*

**BY**

D1608966

**ABBY AYOOLA**

### Copyright 2018 Abby Ayoola

# WHY ARE YOU VEGAN?

"Why are you Vegan?" That's the number one question I get asked all the time and the second question is where do you get your protein from? Any Nigerian who has chosen to live the vegan lifestyle is very familiar with this question. It can even sometimes be an intimidating question as those asking it can often be rather antagonistic when asking. They also will often have their own assumptions about why you chose to be vegan and can be entirely wrong.

The Vegan diet is becoming more and more popular over time, although its proponents are very much still a minority. What are the reasons for the increasing popularity of the Vegan diet? Why do people choose to be Vegan?

In the media today, you can see these reasons popping up over and over. It seems to boil down to about seven main reasons that people are choosing the vegan diet. I find all of the reasons to be reasonable and fascinating. There seems to be something very freeing in following a diet and lifestyle based on conscientious choices. Perhaps it's the reality that when your mind is choosing what you eat rather than your appetite, it gives you a sense of control and power. It allows you to feel that you've taken the reins and are the master of your own destiny. The following seven reasons seem to be primary in this conscious decision making:

## #1 Vegan Reason: Health

Although listed as number one in the list, it may or may not necessarily be the #1 reason people choose veganism. I'm not aware of a study that has been done to determine this rank. However, health is definitely one of the strongest reasons people are choosing the Vegan diet and is one of the most publicized reasons found today in the media-and for good reason. Over and over again, the vegan diet has been proven to be one of the most healthiest diets, if not the most.

## #2 Vegan Reason: Environmental Concerns

Today, more and more people are sharing a growing concern over the destruction of our environment. It is perhaps the greatest concern being discussed. Solutions to the problem are vast and varied, ranging from recycling, to carpooling, to getting rid of the vehicles depending on unrenewable fuels. Interestingly, a Vegan diet ranks very high on ways to reduce your carbon-footprint.

## #3 Vegan Reason: Animal Compassion

One of the most debated reasons for becoming Vegan is also one of the most strongly defended. The topic of animal cruelty is a hot one. Many Vegans may not have health concerns or environmental concerns, but they have a genuine heart for animals and this reason alone is enough for them to make lifelong decisions to avoid any product relying on animals or animal byproducts. They not only adopt a Vegan diet, but also refuse to wear, purchase, endorse, or consume anything that in any way involves animal usage.

## #4 Vegan Reason: Religion and Spirituality

Just as there are many forms of Religion and Spirituality, there are many varied thoughts on what those Religion teaches .Being most familiar with the Christian Religion, I find it interesting that some churches teach that it's Biblical to refrain from an animal-based diet and others teach that the Bible has declared all foods to be acceptable for our diets. It seems the same wide range exists in many other World Religions as well. In Buddhism, some sects lean toward Veganism and some don't. One thing that seems consistent is that the question exists amongst most, if not all, of them.

#### #5 Vegan Reason: Taste Preference

This reason is probably one of the most simple. It comes down to personal preference and, therefore, no-one is right or wrong. Some people like meat and dairy and some people don't. Although a simple reason, it is no less forceful to those who make Vegan choices based upon it.

#### #6 Vegan Reason: Popularity and Uniqueness

More and more, the media is focusing on famous people who are making a turn to Veganism. The more this happens, the more people are following in their footsteps-especially young people. It is becoming more "hip" or non-traditional to break away from the standard "meat and potatoes" diet of the old days and to enter into the sleek and modern ways of Hollywood stars. For some, this reason alone is enough for them to make the change and stick to it.

#### #7 Vegan Reason: Financial

This single reason all by itself is probably not the reason people are changing to a Vegan diet, but it is a factor for many. In many third world countries, meat is a luxury. Often, the diet of these countries is more simple out of necessity and not out of choice. But, here in the United States, we tend to like to save a little money if we can. And those savings can be significant when choosing Vegan ingredients and recipes. This reason may be supplemental, but is a positive one.

So, as you can see there are a wide variety of reasons why I chose to be Vegan. I get protein from beans, lentils, seeds, nuts, green leafy green and seitan. I wrote this book to include Nigerians in the vegan community and to show that you can still enjoy the flavours from Nigeria without compromising your health.

This book is for you if you like your fufu and meat centric foods but you want to eat healthier without compromising on the taste and flavour, if you're vegan but you have no idea how to incorporate nigerian cuisine into your lifestyle, if you're looking to limit the amount of meat and carb in your diet then this book is for you. Nigerian Cuisine is flavourful, full of colours and textures that gels together and that certainly makes you salivate just by the sight alone. Nigerian food will always have a special place in my heart because it's what I grew up on and one of many reasons why I love visiting Nigeria.

**TABLE OF CONTENTS**

SUYA SPICE

PLAINTAIN PUFF

BUNS

WATER YAM SNACK

MOSA

FURA

VEGAN YAM BALL

KOKORO

KULI KULI

BANANA BREAD

STRAWBERRY LEMONADE

## SALADS

AVOCADO SPINACH SALAD

NIGERIAN CHOP SALAD

KALE AND CHICKPEA SALAD

ARUGULA WITH WALNUT SALAD

BEANS AND CORN SALAD

## MEALS

SEITAN FILLET WITH PLAINTAIN WAFFLES

PLAINTAIN NACHOS

FRIED RICE WITH MIXED VEGETABLES

YAM PORRIDGE

IKOKORE

QUICK JOLLOF RICE

EWA AGOYIN

SEITAN FOR BEEF, SUYA AND SPICY SAUCE

MEATLESS SUYA

## SAUCE

ATA DIDI

OKRA AND SPINACH STEW

EFO RIRO

EGUNSI SOUP

BEEF STEW

# Swallows(fufu)

Quinoa

BROCCOLI

Eggplant

CAULIFLOWER

BUTTERNUT SQUASH

Cabbage FuFU

Mushroom Fufu

COCONUT SWALLOW

Bean Sprout SWALLOW

Plaintain Fufu

# SOUP

# CHICKPEA NOODLES SOUP WITH SPINACH

Serves 4

## Ingredients

- 1/2 pack of rice noodles
- 1 can of chickpeas drained and rinsed
- 2 fresh tomatoes (chopped)
- 6 cups of vegetable broth
- 2 cup chopped spinach
- 1 tsp ginger powder
- 1 tsp garlic powder
- 1 tsp turmeric powder
- Salt and pepper to taste
- Fresh parsley for garnishment

## Directions:

Put a pot on the stove on medium high. Add the vegetable broth, tomato and chickpeas.

Cook for 2 minutes, then add the noodles and let cook for 5 minutes.

Add the spinach and spices to the soup, stir it and let simmer for another 2-5 minutes. depending on how you want the texture of your noodles.

Serve your soup and sprinkle parsley on it.

Enjoy your soup.

# RED LENTIL WITH CARROT SOUP

## Ingredients

(serves 4)

- 2 cups red lentils
- 4 cups vegetable stock
- 2 medium sized chopped carrots
- 1 onion diced
- 2 tbsp coconut oil
- 1 clove crushed garlic
- 2 tbsp curry powder
- 1 tbsp cumin
- 1 tsp turmeric
- Juice from ½ of lemon
- Salt and pepper to taste

## Directions:

On medium heat, place your pot on the stove, Add the coconut oil, then add onion cook for about 2 minutes.

Add the garlic and cook for 1 minute.Add the vegetable stock, then the lentils, simmer for 15 minutes.Add all the other ingredients and simmer for another 5 minutes or until the lentils are soft to your desired texture. Serve hot with your favourite bread.

# TOMATO AND BASIL SOUP

## Ingredients
## (serves 1-2)

- 3 large tomatoes (halved)
- 1 cup of vegetable broth
- ½ red bell pepper
- 1 clove of garlic
- 1 cup shredded lettuce
- ½ cup of basil
- 2 tbsp olive oil
- 1 tsp dried thyme
- Salt and pepper to taste
- Fresh coriander for garnish

Direction:

Place a soup point on the stove on medium high heat.

Add all the ingredients to the pot and let simmer for 15 minutes.

Transfer all the ingredients from the pot to a blender.

Blend until smooth.

Serve hot with coriander.

## 3 BEAN SOUP

**Ingredients**
**(serves 4)**

- ½ red bell pepper diced
- 1/2 onion diced
- 4 cups vegetable broth
- 1 can black beans
- 1 can pinto beans
- 1 can red kidney beans
- 1 tsp cumin
- 1 tsp ginger powder
- 1 tsp pepper
- 1 tsp paprika
- 2 tsp garlic powder
- 1 tsp onion powder
- Salt and pepper to taste

Directions:

1. Heat stove-top to medium high heat.
2. In a large pot, saute the diced onions and red pepper until onions go clear. Add broth.
3. Drain and rinse all the beans and add them to the pot.
4. Mix the pot continually so it doesn't burn.

5. Add the cumin, salt, pepper, paprika, garlic, onion and ginger powder and mix until well combined. Bring soup to a boil and simmer for about 7 minutes.

6. Serve warm

## SWEET POTATO QUINOA SOUP

**Ingredients**

**Serves 4**

- 4 cups of vegetable stock
- 2 sweet potatoes (chopped into bite-size pieces)
- 1 red bell pepper chopped
- 4 carrots (chopped)
- 1 cup of broccoli
- 1 cup of celery
- 1 can of white beans
- 1 cup of quinoa
- 1 tbsp sunflower oil
- 1 tsp cumin
- Salt and pepper to taste

Direction:

Heat stove top to medium heat.

Place all the ingredients in a large cooking pot and simmer on a low heat for 40 minutes.

Serve hot and enjoy.

## BUTTERNUT SQUASH SOUP

### Ingredients
### Serves 4

1 medium butternut squash, peeled and cut into cubes

- 4 cups vegetable stock
- 3/4 cup coconut milk
- 1 tablespoon coconut oil
- 1 medium onion, diced
- 3 cloves garlic, minced
- 1 teaspoon powdered ginger
- 3/4 teaspoon sea salt
- 1/4 teaspoon black pepper
- 1/2 teaspoon dried thyme leaves

### Directions:

Heat a large pot over medium heat. Add the coconut oil

Add the onion, garlic, ginger, salt and pepper, and thyme, and saute until the onion is soft and transparent

Add the cubed butternut squash and toss in the onion mixture.

Add the vegetable stock and stir to combine.

Add the lid to the pot and bring to a boil over medium-high heat.

Once the soup reaches a boil turn the heat down to medium-low and simmer for about 20 minutes or until the butternut squash is very tender when you pierce it with a fork.

Remove the soup from the heat and add the coconut milk.

Transfer the soup into blender and blend until smooth. Serve immediately.

# NIGERIAN VEGETARIAN PEPPERSOUP

**Serves: 6**

**Ingredients**

- 4 cups vegetable stock
- 6-8 red potatoes peeled and cut into pieces
- 1 large carrot chopped
- 1 small red onion chopped
- 1 tbsp Nigerian pepper soup spice
- 1 tbsp suya spice(see suya spice recipe)
- 1 small red bell pepper chopped
- 1 large habanero pepper chopped
- 1 tsp ginger powder
- 1 tsp onion powder
- 1 tsp thyme
- salt to taste

**Directions**:

Bring a soup pot on medium heat

Put all the ingredients in the pot

Bring to a boil and let simmer for about 20 minutes or until the potatoes are soft. You can add more vegetable stock as needed for the soup.

Taste the soup and adjust the seasoning to your taste.

Enjoy.

# SNACKS

## MOIN MOIN (BAKED BLACK EYE PEAS)

**Ingredients**
**Makes 6-10 ramekins**

- o 2 cups dried and peeled black eye peas (you can get it from your local african store)
- o 1 white onion
- o 1 red bell pepper
- o 1 scotch bonnet pepper
- o 1 ½ cup water
- o 3 tbsp coconut oil
  1 tsp cumin
- o Salt and pepper to taste
- o ramekin

**Direction**:
Pre heat oven to 350 degrees

Put the black eye peas, onion, habanero pepper, red pepper, onion and water into the blender.

Blend until smooth. This might take about 5 minutes
Transfer the mixture to a large bowl and add coconut oil and seasoning.
Grease the ramekins.

Divide the mixture into little ramekins and bake in the oven for about 30 minutes or until it's firmed.

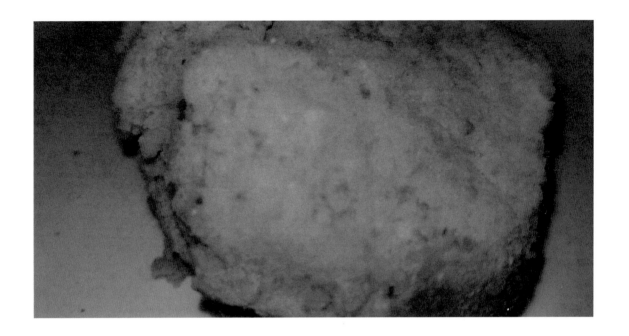

**AKARA( Fried black bean)**

**Ingredients**

- 2 cups dried and peeled black eyed beans
- 1 medium onion
- 1 ¼ cup of water
- 1 large red bell pepper
- 1 scotch bonnet pepper
- 1 tsp cumin
- 1 tsp turmeric
- Salt to taste
- Canola oil for frying

**Directions**:

Blend all the ingredients together in the blender until the mixture is smooth. This might take about 5 minutes.

Transfer the mixture to a large bowl and season with salt.
Heat some oil in a deep fryer or large frying pan.

Add the mixture in spoonfuls, making sure to avoid overcrowding the pan. Fry until golden brown on both sides and drain on some kitchen paper.

You can eat it with ogi (pap) or as a sandwich between 2 slices of bread.
 Enjoy!

# NIGERIAN VEGGIE GROUND PIE
## MAKES 12

## Ingredients

### The filling

1 pack veggie grounds

1 cup sliced oyster mushrooms

1 orange pepper diced

1 onion sliced

2 scotch bonnet peppers chopped

1 medium yukon potato diced

½ cup diced carrots

2 tbsp coconut oil

1 tsp thyme

1 vegetable cube

1 tsp oregano

1 tsp black pepper

1 tsp Salt

Additional Salt to taste

### The dough

1 1/2 cups Bread Flour

1 1/2ups All purpose flour

1 tbsp baking powder

3 tbsp cold vegan butter

½ tsp salt

¼ cup apple sauce

1 tsp date syrup

**Direction**:

**To make the filling**

Saute the mushrooms with 1 tsp of salt and the coconut oil in a saute pan on medium heat. Saute about 10 minutes.

Once the mushrooms have browned, add in the onions, scotch bonnet peppers, thyme, oregano, black pepper and vegetable cube and continue to saute until the onions are softened and translucent.

Once the onions have softened, add in the carrots, potatoes and veggie ground. Turn the heat down to low and continue to saute for another 10 minutes or until the potatoes are tender. Toss in the bell peppers and continue to saute for another 5 minutes then turn the heat off and set aside.

**To make the Pie dough**

Preheat your oven to 350 degrees
In a bowl, combine the bread and all purpose flour, baking powder, and salt. Gently cut in the vegan butter in chunks

Add the applesauce to the flour and butter mixture and mix with a wooden spoon to bring the dough together. Add in some ice cold water 1 tbsp at a time until the dough comes together, be sure not to add too much water at once.

Knead the dough together on a floured surface, cover and let rest in the refrigerator for about 30 minutes or until you are ready to use it.

### To make the pies

Cut the rested dough into 12 even pieces. Taking one piece of dough at a time, roll it out into a circle and place about 2 tablespoons of the filling on half the dough circle. Use the other half to cover the filling and seal the edges of the dough by crimping with a fork. To ensure a secure seal, brush the edges of the dough circle with water before close and sealing.

Prepare all the pies and using a fork gently poke the tops of the pie to create air vents and prevent the pies from bursting open. Mix the date syrup with teaspoons of water, and lightly brush the tops of the dough to glaze the pies.

Place the pies on a parchment lined baking sheet and bake in the preheated oven for 25-30 minutes.

Enjoy.

**VEGAN AGEGE BREAD**

**INGREDIENTS**

½ cup of bread flour

1/2 cup vegan butter

1 ½ cup apple sauce

1/2 teaspoon salt

½ cup sifted organic coconut flour

1 teaspoon baking powder

**DIRECTION**:

Pre-heat oven to 350 degrees

1) Mix together butter, apple sauce

2) Combine the flours, salt, baking powder and whisk thoroughly into batter until there are no lumps.

3) Pour into greased loaf pan and bake at 350 degrees for 40 minutes.

4) Remove from pan and cool on rack.

## BANANA-LIME FRITTERS

4 ripe bananas

6 tablespoons plain flour

1 tablespoon sugar

1 tsp cinnamon powder

pinch of salt

1 tbsp arrowroot powder

1 lime, zest finely-grated

½ cup rice milk

1 teaspoon Vegan  butter

oil, for frying

icing sugar, for dusting

### Direction:

Sift together the flour, sugar, arrowroot powder, cinnamon and salt into a large bowl.

Stir to combine then add the milk, butter and bananas

Beat with a wire whisk until the batter is smooth.

Gently fold into the batter along with the lime zest.

Heat the oil in a pan. When hot fry the batter 1 tbsp at time.

Fry until nicely browned and heated through.

Remove with a slotted spoon and drain on kitchen paper as you cook the remaining  batter Serve hot, dusted with icing sugar

# CHIN CHIN

## Ingredients

- 2 cups all purpose flour
- 1/2 cup dates sugar
- 1/2 tsp baking powder
- 1 tsp nutmeg
- 1 tsp cinnamon powder
- 2 tbsp canola oil
- 1/4 cup almond milk

**Direction**:

Pre-heat oven to 350 degrees

Place the flour, sugar, baking powder, nutmeg and cinnamon in a large mixing bowl and combine all the ingredients.

Add the oil and a little bit of the milk and mix with spoon. Start to add the milk a little at a time until you have a firm dough. You don't want it to be too sticky so it won't be hard to roll out. Knead the dough for a couple of minutes then wrap it and refrigerate for 30 mins.

Place the dough on a lightly floured surface and roll out until it is about 1 cm thick.

Cut the dough into strips and then little squares.

Place the squares on a baking tray lined with parchment paper.

Bake in a pre-heated oven for 10 minutes until golden brown.

# HUMMUS WITH SWEET POTATO FLATBREAD

**Ingredients**

**(serves 2)**

> 1 canned chickpeas
>
> 2 cloves garlic

- ¼ cup tahini
- Juice of 1/2 a lemon

> 2 tbsp olive oil

- ½ tsp cumin
- Pinch of salt

## DIRECTION FOR THE HUMMUS

Place all the ingredients in the blender and blend until smooth.
Set aside.

### For the flatbread:

¾ cup sweet potato, cooked and mashed

1 cup all-purpose flour

3 tbsp vegan butter

**Directions**:

In a mixing bowl, add the mashed sweet potato, butter and the flour and stir until well-combined. Use your hands to form a dough ball. It should not be too sticky.

Separate the dough ball into 5 equal parts. Dust your working surface with flour and roll out each tortilla with a rolling pin. Don't make them too thin, otherwise they won't be as soft and flexible.

Place the tortillas in a hot pan over medium-high heat and cook for 1 minute on both sides. Stack the cooked tortillas on a plate covered with a clean kitchen towel while you cook the rest. This will allow them to stay very flexible and soft.

# RASPBERRY NICE CREAM CAKE

## Serves 4
## INGREDIENTS

- 3 frozen sliced bananas
- ½ cup frozen raspberries
- 1 cup frozen Strawberries
- ½ cup frozen blueberries
  1 can of coconut milk
- Garnish with any topping of choice

### Directions

Add all ingredients to a high speed blender.

Blend until smooth and creamy.

Pour the nice cream on a parchment paper and put it in a cake pan

freeze for an hour before serving.

Sprinkle with topping of choice

Enjoy!

**Caramel popped corn(guguru)**

**Serves 4**

14 cups popped popcorn

1/4 cup date syrup

1 cup brown sugar

1/2 teaspoon salt

1/2 cup vegan butter

1/2 teaspoon baking soda

2 teaspoons vanilla extract

**Direction:**

You can get the corn kernels from any grocery store.

Pre heat oven to 200 degrees

Place the popped popcorn into a large bowl and set aside.

Combine the brown sugar, date syrup, butter and salt in a large saucepan on low-med heat. Bring the mixture to a boil only stirring enough to blend through. Boil for about 4 minutes.

Remove from the heat and add the baking soda and vanilla. It will lighten in color and become foamy. Immediately pour over your popcorn and mix through. Transfer to baking sheets and place in the oven.

Bake for one hour, mixing it every 15 minutes.

Allow to cool completely before you break it apart.

Serve with topping of choice like peanuts, almonds etc

## GREEN MATCHA NICE CREAM

### Ingredients

(serves 4)

- 4 sliced and frozen bananas
- 1 pitted dates

1 tbsp matcha green powder

- Topping of your choice

### Direction:

Place the frozen bananas, matcha and date in a blender

Blend for about 1 minute or until you get an ice cream consistency

Scoop into a bowl and serve with your favourite toppings.

# NIGERIAN DOUGHNUT

**Serves 4**

1¼ cups all-purpose flour

2 tablespoons warm water

½ teaspoon active dry yeast

2 teaspoons applesauce

1 tablespoon brown sugar

3 tablespoons rice milk

1 teaspoon apple cider vinegar

1 teaspoon baking soda

3 tablespoons very hot water

3/4 cup canola oil for frying

Icing sugar (for sprinkling)

**Direction**:

In a small bowl, combine the 2 tbsp warm water, active dry yeast, and pinch of sugar, set aside until foamy that usually takes 5 minutes.

While the yeast is setting, whisk together the applesauce, sugar, milk, and apple cider vinegar plus baking soda in a bowl. Add the 3tbsp hot water and mix.

Add the activated yeast mixture and whisk until combined.

Stir in the flour until combined. Cover the dough and let rest for at least an hour.

In a frying pan, add the canola oil over medium high heat. Roll out the dough to about 1/8 to 1/4 inch thickness, cut the dough into 1-2 inch squares.

When the oil is hot enough, drop dough in, make sure you don't crowd the beignets. Make sure you stay close as they fry, the first side will cook very quickly (1-2 min), turn each beignet over when first side is cooked and ensure the other side fries as well (additional 1-2 min). Remove from oil with a slotted spoon and transfer to a paper tower plate.

When all the donuts are cooked, sprinkle with powdered sugar and enjoy.

**STRAWBERRY Muffins**

**Makes 12 muffins**

**Ingredients**

1 cup all purpose  flour

1 1/2 tsp baking powder

1/2 tsp ground cinnamon

1/8 tsp sea salt

1 tsp lemon zest

3/4 cup unsweetened almond milk

3 tbsp peanut butter

3 tbsp unsweetened applesauce

3 tbsp date syrup

1/2 tsp vanilla extract

1/4 tsp almond extract

1/4 cup strawberry  jam

**Directions**

Preheat oven to 375 degrees.

 Oil the muffin pan so it won't stick and set aside.

In a mixing bowl whisk together the flour, baking powder, cinnamon, lemon zest and salt.

In a separate mixing bowl whisk together the almond milk, peanut butter, applesauce, date syrup and extracts until smooth.

Pour the wet ingredients in with the dry and stir together with a rubber spatula just until combined. Add the jam and mix well.

Scoop equally into 12 muffin pan.

Bake the muffins for 10-12 minutes or until a toothpick inserted into one comes out clean.

Cool the muffins for a couple minutes in the pan before removing them onto a cooling rack to cool completely

## Suya Spice

- 5 tablespoons crushed peanuts or grounded kuli kuli or peanut butter powder.
- 5 tablespoons ginger powder
- 2 tablespoons hot chili pepper
- 1 tsp onion powder
- 1 tsp garlic powder
- 1 tbsp paprika
- ½ teaspoon salt

**Direction:**

If you're using roasted groundnut, simply grind roasted groundnuts, squeeze out the oil from them with a paper towel or napkin, dry fry it on the stove to take out the oil completely. It's very important that the grounded peanuts doesn't have any oil. If using kuli kuli just blend it and if you're using the peanut powder you don't need any extra step.

Combine all the ingredients in a bowl.

Blend all the ingredients together

When done, sift the spice with a sifter to make it less clumpy.

**Use for Meatless Seitan Suya.**

## Plantain Puff Puff

### Ingredients

- 2 large overripe plantains
- 3 cups all-purpose flour
- 2 1/4 teaspoons active dry yeast
- 11/2 cup warm water
- 1/2 teaspoon salt
  ½ tsp nutmeg
- ½ teaspoon ginger powder

**Direction:**

Pour half a cup of warm water into a large bowl. Add in your yeast and set aside. Peel the plantains and blend together with remaining 1 cup of water until smooth. Alternately, you could mash the plantains in a bowl with a fork then add the water and stir to combine.

Pour blended plantains into yeast mixture. Add salt and ginger and stir well. Add in flour in little bits, stirring each time you add some. Stir to form a batter. You should be able to hold the batter in your hands without it falling out quickly. If it is too light, add more flour. If it is too thick, add more water.

Cover the batter with plastic wrap and let it rest for about 40 minutes.
Heat oil in a large pot for 5-10 minutes on medium heat. Drop tablespoons of batter into the oil to fry. Be careful not to overcrowd the pan. Let the balls cook for about 5-10 minutes until golden brown.

Flip the sides half-way through. Remove and place on paper towel to absorb excess oil.
Enjoy.

# Buns

- 2 cups All purpose flour
- ½ tsp baking powder
- ¼ cup sugar
- ½ tsp grated nutmeg
- Flax egg(2 tbsp flax seed with 6 tbsp water)
- 4tbsp Oil or melted vegan butter
- ¼ cup Water
- 3 tbsp rice  milk

## Direction

1. Combine all the dry ingredients (flour, baking powder, salt, nutmeg and sugar) in a bowl.

2. In another bowl, combine the "wet ingredients" (flax egg, water, oil or butter and milk) together.

3. Mix the wet ingredients into the dry ingredients to make your dough. You can use your hands, a fork or a wooden spoon to combine the ingredients. You want a rough consistency. Be sure to not overwork your dough.

4. Heat your oil on medium heat. Do not start frying the buns until the oil is properly hot. You don't want it too hot either, or the outside will get done quick, leaving the inside raw

5. Use an ice cream scoop to shape the buns. Simply dip the scoop in oil(to prevent sticking) and scoop the dough into the hot oil.

6. When you drop the dough in the oil, it'll sink to the bottom. Make sure you start stirring and turning the buns immediately.

7. When the buns are getting done, they will float to the top. They will no longer be submerged in the oil, and you will see cracks in the skin.

# Water Yam Fritters(ojojo)

- 1 whole piece of water yam (peeled, washed and grated using the cheese grater
- ½ finely chopped red onions
- ¼ cup red bell pepper
- 1 chopped scotch bonnet
- 1 vegetable cube

  Salt to taste

**Direction**

Add the chopped onion, , bell pepper, scotch bonnet, and vegetable cube to the grated water yam. thoroughly mix all ingredients together with your hands. Add a small quantity of salt and mix again. Heat some oil in a deep base pot or pan because the water yam fritter has to be deep fried.

Check the oil is hot enough by dropping a small portion of the grated yam into the oil. If it rises to the top almost immediately, then its ready.

Using an ice cream scooper, scoop the graded yam into the hot oil and fry for about 4 minutes or until golden brown.

Remove fried yam fritter from the oil and allow to drain over some kitchen towel.

Best served hot.

## MOSA

### Ingredients

- 1 ripe plantain
- 4 tbsp all purpose flour
½ tsp nutmeg
- Salt to taste
- Canola oil

Direction:
Place the ripe plantain in a large mixing bowl and mash to form a smooth purée. Add the rest of the dry ingredients.

Heat some canola oil in a frying pan and add the mixture one tablespoon at a time. Make sure not to over crowd the pan. Fry on medium heat, turning over once or twice to brown both sides.
Drain on some kitchen paper and serve hot or warm.

## Fura

- 1/2 cup Millet
- 1 teaspoon Dried pepper (ground)
- 1 teaspoon garlic powder
- 1 teaspoon African black pepper (ground)
- 1 teaspoon Dry ginger root (ground)
- 1 tablespoon Corn flour
- 2 liter water
- 1 litre Coconut yogurt
- Sugar to taste

## Direction

- Mix the flours(except corn flour) with all the spices thoroughly. Add a little water and mix to form a thick paste. Mold into medium sized balls.
- In a medium pot on medium heat, Boil the water for about 5 minutes. Add the balls to the boiling water and continue boiling for about 20 minutes.
- Remove the balls from the boiling pot and pound thoroughly. Mold into small balls and sprinkle corn flour to keep the balls moist.
- Serve mashed with coconut yoghurt and sugar to taste.

## Vegan Yam Ball

- ½ white yam
- 5 white mushrooms
- ½ onion chopped
- 1 tbsp tomato puree
- Fresh chopped spinach
- ½ tbsp coconut oil
- ½ scotch bonnet
- 1 clove of garlic
- Spice 1 tsp each( thyme, salt, onion powder and paprika and turmeric)

### Directions

1. In a medium pot on medium heat add 6 cups of water with 2 tbsp salt to boil the yam until soft.

2. In a saucepan over medium heat add coconut oil, onion, garlic, scotch bonnet and mushroom and cook for 3 minutes

3. Add tomato paste and spices, cook 2 minutes

4. Add spinach and cook for another 4 minutes. Set aside

5. Take the cooked yam, pour the water out and transfer it into a bowl

6. Mash the yam with potato masher until stretchy.

7. Roll the mashed yam in a small ball, flatten it, make a little dent in the middle so the filling can fit.

8. Put the filling, roll another ball, flatten it and put it on top of the ball with the filling to close. Roll into a ball.

9. Shallow fry until golden brown on both sides. Enjoy.

# Kokoro

## Ingredients

- ½ cup corn meal
- 1/8 cup millet flour
- 1 cup all purpose flour
- 2 tbsp sugar
- oil for deep frying
- Pinch of salt
- 1 cup of water

## Direction

- Pour 1 cup of water into a pot, leave to boil.
- In a medium sized bowl, mix the corn meal, flours, sugar and salt together

- Gently add ½ of the corn and flour mixture into the boiling water and stir, make sure there are no lumps.
- Remove the pot from the stove. Leave the mixture to cool
- Once cooled, add the rest of the flour mixture and mix.
- Transfer the dough to a bowl and knead until it becomes firm.
- Take a portion of the dough and roll out on a flat surface until you get a long stick.
- Repeat until all the dough is accounted for.
- Pour the oil into a skillet and let it heat up.
- Fry the rolled kokoro until golden brown.
- Enjoy.

# Kuli kuli

## Ingredients

1 cup dry roasted groundnut or peanuts

½ tbsp grated ginger

1 tsp garlic powder

¼ tsp onion powder

peanut oil for frying

## Directions

Blend roasted groundnuts and ginger, onion powder and garlic until smooth

Squeeze the groundnut paste to remove any excess oil.

Mold the paste into any shape that you want.

Heat the oil on medium heat in a frying pan, fry until it's brown and hard

Enjoy

**P.S this is the main ingredient for suya spice..**

# Banana Bread

**Serves 4**

## Ingredients

- 3 Medium brown riped bananas
- 2 cups all purpose flour
- ¼ cup apple sauce
- 1/2 cup Rolled Oats
- 1/2 cup Coconut Sugar
- 1/4 cup sunflower butter
- 2 tbsp Ground Flax plus 6 tbsp Water
- 2 tsp Baking Powder
- 1 tsp Baking Soda
- 2 tsp Apple Cider Vinegar
- 1 tsp Vanilla Extract
- 1/2 tsp Salt

**Directions:**

Preheat your oven to 350F.

In a small bowl, combine the ground flax with 6 tbsp water to form an "egg." Stir and set aside for 5-10 minutes.

Place the flour into a medium sized bowl and add the baking powder, baking soda, rolled oats and salt. Mix well and set aside.

Add bananas to a separate, large bowl, and mash with a fork until they form an even, runny texture. Add the Nut Butter, Coconut Sugar, Apple Cider Vinegar, Vanilla Extract, and flax egg and apple sauce. Mix well.

Slowly incorporate the dry flour mixture into the wet Banana mixture, stirring well and until all clumps have dissolved.

Pour the batter into a parchment paper-lined or greased 8″ bread pan, smoothing the top off with a spatula.

Bake at 350F for 45 minutes, or until the top is golden brown, and a toothpick comes out cleanly or with minimal crumbs. Remove from the oven and let cool for 10 minutes in the pan, then remove from the pan and allow to cool completely before slicing.

## STRAWBERRY LEMONADE

1 cup fresh raspberries

2 cups fresh strawberries

8 cups of alkaline or distilled water

1 cup date syrup

2 cups fresh squeezed lemon juice

sliced strawberries, lemons, limes and mint for garnish

## Directions

Blend the raspberries and strawberries in a blender with 2 cups of the water. Blend until smooth.

Combine the strawberry puree, syrup, water mixture, lemon juice and remaining 6 cups of water in a pitcher.

Stir thoroughly then chill until ready to serve. Just before serving, stir in sliced strawberries, lemon, lime and mint sprigs.

Enjoy.

# SALADS

## AVOCADO AND SPINACH SALAD

- 2 ripe avocados
- 2 large ripe tomatoes
- 1 Tbsp fresh lemon juice
- 1 cup of baby spinach
- 2 tbsp olive oil
- 3 tbsp vegan cheese
- 3 Tbsp. chopped cilantro
- 2 tbsp fresh parsley chopped
- salt and pepper to taste
- Olives for garnishment

### Directions

Cut the avocado, tomato in chunks. Add the spinach

Add lemon juice, oil, cilantro, parsley, salt, and pepper.

Stir together and serve. Garnish with olive.

# NIGERIAN CHOP SALAD

Ingredients
Serves 4

4 medium sized carrots
½ of small white onion
1 medium bunch of lettuce
1 medium bunch of cabbage
½ cup of green Peas
4 Medium sized roma tomatoes
2 pieces of cucumber
1 can of Baked Beans in tomato sauce
1 can of corn
1/2 cup of vegan mayonnaise
½ cup coconut yogurt

DIRECTIONS:
Chop the carrot, cabbage, lettuce, tomato, cucumber, onion
Put it in a big salad bowl. Add the peas and corn.
Drain the tomato sauce from the beans and add the beans to the salad bowl.

For the sauce
Add the coconut yogurt and mayonnaise together In a separate bowl
Add the sauce to the salad bowl and toss together.
Serve and enjoy

# KALE AND CHICKPEA SALAD

**Serves 4 people**

## Ingredients

4 cups of chopped kale

½ cup of cooked chickpeas

¼ sundried tomatoes

Creamy dressing of choice

## Direction

Toss all the ingredients in a salad bowl

# ARUGULA SALAD WITH WALNUT

**Serves 4**

**Ingredients**

4 cups arugula

½ cup of walnut

½ cup of cherry tomato

Direction:

Toss all the ingredients together in a bowl

Enjoy.

# BEAN AND CORN SALAD

½ cup of diced red peppers

1 can of sweetcorn

I cup of cooked Nigerian red beans

1 tbsp olive oil

2-3 tbsp freshly squeezed lime juice

Coriander for garnishment

**Direction**

Toss all the ingredients together and enjoy

# MEALS

**SEITAN FILLET WIITH PLANTAIN WAFFLES**

**For the Seitan Fillet**

1  can of chickpeas

¼ cup nutritional yeast

1/2 cup vital wheat gluten

3 tbsp vegetable broth

1 teaspoon liquid smoke

2 tsp all purpose seasoning

1/2 cup cornstarch

Oil, for frying

**For the Waffles:**

3 large ripe plantain

2½ Tablespoons coconut oil, melted

1 tsp vanilla extract

1 tsp cinnamon

1 tsp apple cider vinegar

½ Teaspoon sea salt

1/8 tsp baking powder

½ Teaspoon baking soda

**DIRECTION:**

SEITAN FILLET

Drain the chickpeas, and pour into a large mixing bowl. Mash pretty well, with a potato masher or a fork. You want a little texture, but mostly all mashed.

Add the vital wheat gluten, the broth, nutritional yeast and all the seasonings. Mash all together, Mash and knead slightly until everything is combined and forms a dough.

Shape into fillets

Heat about 1-1 1/2 inches of oil in a pan

Dip the fillet in the cornstarch, and pat off excess. Once oil is hot, fry on each side for a few minutes until golden brown on each side.

**Waffles:**

Plug in your waffle maker and let it heat up.

Peel the plantains and chop them each into 4 pieces.

Place the plantain pieces in a high speed blender and blend until smooth

Add the oil to the plantains and blend again, until completely pureed.

Add the cinnamon, vanilla and apple cider vinegar to the blender. Blend again on high for a few seconds to mix well.

Add the salt, baking powder and baking soda to the blender. blend again to mix all the ingredients together.

Oil your waffle iron and place ⅓-1/4 cup of batter into the center of your waffle iron, depending on the size of your waffle maker.

Cook until the waffle is browned to your liking, and repeat until you cook all the batter. Be sure to keep the waffle maker oiled before each waffle.

Assemble your waffles with the seitan fillet and top with maple syrup or any topping of your choice.

## PLANTAIN NACHOS

INGREDIENTS

PLANTAINS:
2 green plantains
2 tablespoon coconut oil, melted

### GUACAMOLE
2 avocados , diced
1/4 cup red onion , chopped
1 tsp garlic powder
2 tablespoons fresh cilantro , chopped
Juice  of ½ a lime
salt to taste

PICO DE GALLO
2 fresh Roma tomatoes , chopped
2 tablespoons red onion , chopped
2 tablespoon fresh cilantro , chopped
1/2 lime , juice of
1/4 fresh jalapeno , minced
salt to taste

CREAMY SAUCE

1/4 cup mayonnaise

1 clove garlic , peeled

squeeze of fresh lime juice

salt to taste

**Direction**:

Preheat oven to 350F. Cover two large baking sheets with parchment paper and set aside.

Prep the plantains. Cut off both ends of the plantain, then with the tip of a sharp knife, make shallow slits lengthwise along the skin. Use your fingers to pry off the strips, slice the plantains into coin size circles. Use two spoon to toss the slices in a large bowl with the melted coconut oil.

Bake the plantains. Use four coins to make each nacho piece. Lay them flat on the baking sheet, sprinkle with salt. Bake for about 30 minutes until very crisp and beginning to brown. Remove from the oven.

PICO DE GALLO

Stir together all ingredients in a medium bowl. Season with salt to taste.

GUACAMOLE

Stir together all ingredients in a medium bowl. Mash until desired consistency. Season with salt to taste.

CREAMY SAUCE

Combine all ingredients in the bowl of a food processor. Pulse until smooth. Season with salt to taste.

# FRIED RICE WITH MIXED VEGETABLE

## Ingredients
## (serves 2)

- 2 cup par broiled rice
- ½ white onion
- 2 cups of vegetable stock
- ½ cup of mixed vegetables
- ½ cup corn
- 3 tbsp vegan butter
- 1/2 tsp dried thyme
- 1 tbsp curry powder
- salt and pepper to taste

Direction:

Heat the butter in a cooking pot and sauté the chopped onion for a few seconds. Add the rice and the vegetable stock.

Add the curry powder, thyme, and season with salt and pepper. Stir, cover with a lid and turn the heat to low medium heat. When the water is almost dried out stir in the the mixed vegetables and cook for a few more minutes to allow the vegetables to gel with the rice.

# YAM PORRIDGE

## Ingredients:

- 1 medium size yam (peeled and cubed)
- 1 cup blended pepper mix (1 bell pepper 1 scotch bonnet)
- 1 small onion (finely chopped)
- 1 cup chopped kale
- 1 clove garlic (chopped)
- 3 Tablespoon palm oil
- 1 tsp garlic powder
- 1 tsp ginger powder
- 1 tsp onion powder
- 1 cube vegetable maggi
- Salt to taste

**Directions:**

Heat up the oil in a large pot; add in the chopped onion and garlic. Stir continuously until the onion is cooked

Add in the blended peppers, 1.5 cups water, maggi, salt.

Cover and cook for 5-6 minutes

Add in the cocoyam, Simmer on below medium heat for 25-30mins. Combine.

Taste and adjust for seasoning

Add in the chopped vegetables if using, combine.

Remove from heat and serve with your choice of protein

# Ikokore(water yam porridge)

**This recipe holds a special place in my heart. I am an Ijebu girl from Sagamu, Ogun state. Ikokore is a dish that's associated with ijebus and I love every bit of it. Whenever I go back to Sagamu, my late mom and my grandma always make sure they cook it for me everyday.**

## Ingredients

- 1 lb or half of water Yam (Peeled and grated)..
- 4 Nori Sheets( crumbled)
- 1/2 onion
- 1 fresh tomato
- 1 habanero pepper
- 2 cups water
- 3 tbsp coconut oil
- 1 vegetable cube
- Salt to taste

## Direction:

1. Blend the onion, scotch bonnet, tomato with 1 cup of water.
2. Heat up coconut oil in a pot and add 1 cup water, blended pepper, tomato and onion mixture
3. Add nori sheets crumbled
4. Add salt and or vegetable cube
5. Bring to a quick boil and reduce heat to simmer
6. Gently scoop in into the sauce grated water yam with a spoon, 1 tbsp at a time.
7. Cover and slow cook till water yam lumps are soft and tender.
8. Let rest for 5 minutes before serving.

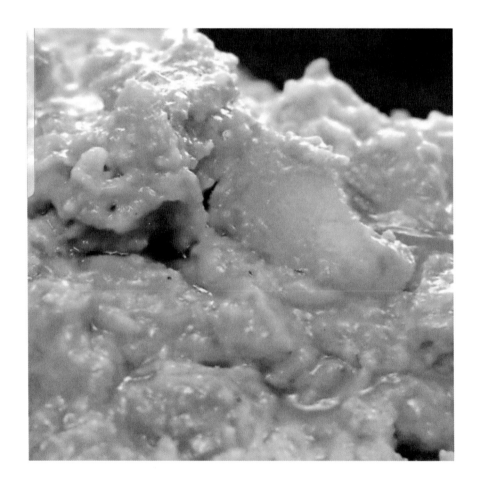

## Quick Jollof Rice

- 3 tablespoons vegetable oil
- 1 cup uncooked long-grain rice
- 1 teaspoon garlic salt
- 1/2 teaspoon ground cumin
- 1/4 cup chopped onion
- 1/2 cup tomato sauce
- 1 scotch bonnet
- 1 bell pepper
- 2 cups vegetable broth
- Salt to taste

**Direction:**

Blend tomato sauce, scotch bonnet and bell pepper in a blender. Set aside.

Heat oil in a large saucepan over medium heat and add rice. Cook, stirring constantly, until puffed and golden. While rice is cooking, sprinkle with salt and cumin.

Stir in onions and cook until tender. Stir in blended tomato sauce and vegetable broth; bring to a boil. Reduce heat to low, cover and simmer for 20 to 25 minutes. Fluff with a fork.

Enjoy.

# Ewa Agoyin

**Ingredients:**

**The Beans:**

- 2 cups Red or White beans
- Salt to taste

**The Sauce:**

- ½ cup of canola oil
- 4 medium bell peppers
- 3 red dried chilies
- 1 purple onion(2 halves)
- 1 tbsp cayenne pepper
- 2 scotch bonnets
- 1 tbsp ground sea weed
- 1 vegetable cube
- Salt to taste

**Directions:**

**To Prepare the Beans:**

•Wash the beans under running water

•Add 6 cups of water to a pot, set on high heat and bring to a boil.

•Add the beans and reduce the heat to minimum.

•Leave on low heat for 2 hours or until the beans is very soft.

•Add salt to taste. Mash up the beans with potato masher.

**To Prepare the Sauce: (Agoyin pepper)**

•In a blender, combine the bell pepper, ½ onion, scotch bonnet and peppers with a bit of water. Puree to a coarse texture. Pour the pureed peppers into a sieve to get rid of excess water.

•Set a medium sized pot on medium heat, add the canola oil and wait for the oil to get heated

•Add in chopped ½ onion, vegetable cube, seaweed and cayenne pepper, stir at interval until the onion is caramelized. This takes about 20-25 minutes.

•Add the sieved pepper, seaweed salt and vegetable cube.Stir. Cover and leave to fry for another 15 to 20 minutes or until the sauce is darkened

Serve with the beans and enjoy.

# Seitan For Beef Stew, Suya, Sweet and Spicy sauce

## Ingredients

### For the Dough For Beef Stew
- 1 cup vital wheat gluten
- 1/4 cup chickpea flour
- 1 cup water

### For the dough for Suya Beef
- 1 cup of Vital Wheat Gluten
- ¼ nutritional yeast
- ¼ chickpea flour
- 1 tbsp suya spice
- 1 tbsp peanut powder
- 1 cup of water

### For the dough of sweet and spicy chicken
- 1 cup of Vital wheat gluten
- ¼ oyster mushroom grinded
- Spice mix tsp( garlic, onion and paprika and salt)
- 1 cup of water

### For the Broth - Beef Flavor
- 5 1/2 cups low sodium vegetable broth
- 1/2 cup dry red wine
- 1/3 cup soy sauce
- 2 tablespoons vegan Worcestershire sauce
- 1 teaspoon dried thyme
- 1/2 teaspoon onion powder
- 1/2 teaspoon garlic powder

- 1/2 teaspoon black pepper

**For the Broth – Suya flavour**
- 6 cups low sodium vegetable broth or water
- 1/3 cup peanut powder
- 2 teaspoons liquid smoke
- 2 teaspoons smoked paprika
- 1 teaspoon onion powder
- 1 teaspoon garlic powder
- 2 teaspoon ginger powder

**For the Broth - Chicken Flavor**
- 6 cups low sodium vegetable broth
- 1/3 cup soy sauce
- 1/4 cup nutritional yeast flakes
- 1 1/2 teaspoons white wine vinegar
- 1 teaspoon onion powder
- 1/2 teaspoon garlic powder
- 1/2 teaspoon liquid smoke

**Direction:**

Stir the vital wheat gluten and chickpea flour or nutritional yeast or grounded up oyster mushroom together in a medium bowl.

Add the water and stir to form a soft dough.

Transfer the dough to a work surface and knead it for 5 minutes.

Allow the dough to rest for 5 minutes.

While the dough rests, stir all of the broth ingredients for your choice of broth together in a large pot.

Place the pot over high heat and bring the mixture to a boil. Lower the heat to a low simmer.

Cut the dough into smaller strips or chunks.

Add the dough to the broth.

Allow the broth to simmer for 1 hour, uncovered, watching closely to ensure it stays at a low simmer (don't allow it to rapidly boil).

Remove the pot from heat and allow it to cool a bit.

Fry it on the stove with sunflower oil to your desired texture

Use it in a recipe immediately, or refrigerate for up to 5 days, or freeze.

# Meatless Suya

- Fried Suya Seitan (check suya seitan recipe)
- Suya spice (check suya spice recipe
- Peanut oil about 2 tbsp

## Direction

- pre- heat oven to 350 degrees
- Add all the ingredients together in a bowl
- Combine very well
- Pour the suya mixture into a baking pan
- Bake for 5-7 minutes in the oven

# STEW

## ATA DIDI

### Ingredients

- 1 tbsp coconut oil
- 2 large bell pepper
- 2 sweet pepper
- 3 scotch bonnet
- ½ onion, chopped
- 1 vegetable cube

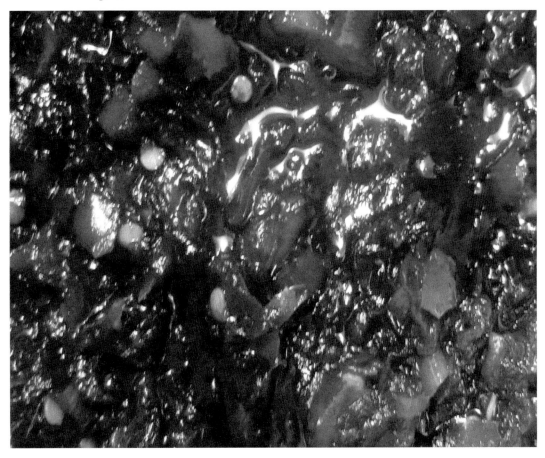

## Direction

1. Blend bell, sweet and scotch bonnet in a blender with a little bit of water
2. Pass the blended mixture through a sifter to remove excess water
3. On a medium sauce pan on medium high heat put in coconut oil and fry the onion for about 5 minutes
4. Add the pepper mixture, vegetable cube and salt to taste
5. Cook for about 10 minutes.
6. ENJOY with rice, yam or with beans.

## Okra and Spinach Stew

- 16 okras(lady fingers) chopped
- 1 pack of frozen spinach or fresh spinach
- 1 cup sliced mushroom
- 1 onion
- 1-2 Cayenne pepper
- 1 tsp sea salt
- 1 tsp turmeric
- 1 tsp curry
- 1 tsp thyme
- ½ tbsp coconut oil.
- 2 cups of hot water

**Direction**

- In a medium sauce pan over medium heat, add oil then onion
- Cook for 2 minutes. Add the chopped okra and stir, cook for 2 minutes.
- Add the hot water, spices and stir thoroughly
- Add the mushroom, stir occasionally and cook for 8 minutes
- Add the spinach, cover the pot and let simmer for 2 minutes.
- Serve with your favourite swallow(fufu)

**Efo Riro**

- 1 pack of frozen spinach
- ½ cup grounded melon seed
- 1 onion
- 1 scotch bonnet
- 3 red bell peppers
- 1 pack of mushroom
- 1 cup cooked seitan( see recipe for beef seitan)
- 1 tsp each(salt, paprika, turmeric, onion powder and garlic powder)
- 1 tbsp coconut oil

**Directions**

- Blend bell pepper, scotch bonnet and ½ of the onion.
- Cook mushroom in little oil and set aside.
- Use the rest of the oil on a medium size pot on medium heat. Add the other ½ onion chopped and melon seed.
- Cook for 5 minutes. Add blended pepper, spices, mushroom and seitan.
- Cook for 2 minutes
- Add spinach and let simmer for 4 minutes.
- Serve with favourite swallow or rice.

## Egunsi Soup

- 2 cups of grounded egunsi seed(melon)
- 1 can of young jackfruit in salt water(drained and rinsed)
- 2 tomatoes
- 3 cup of water
- 4 sheets of seaweed, crushed
- 1 ½ onion
- 1 scotch bonnet
- 1 bell pepper
- 1 pack of frozen spinach
- 2 tbsp coconut oil
- 1 tsp each (paprika, salt, curry and thyme)

## Direction

1. Remove and discard any seed from the jackfruit
2. Cut off the hard core part and break the jackfruit on small pieces .
3. In a medium sauce pan, over medium heat add 1 tbsp of oil and fry 1/2 onion.
4. Add the jackfruit and cook for 6 minutes and set aside.
5. Add a little bit of water to the egunsi to form a paste and set aside.
6. Blend the bell pepper, scotch bonnet, ½ onion, tomato with 1 cup of water until smooth.
7. Pass the blended ingredients through a sifter to remove excess water.
8. In a medium size saucepan over medium heat, add 1 tbsp of oil and ½ chopped onion
9. Add the drained blended ingredients and spices. Mix and let cook for 10 minutes
10. Add the cooked jackfruit and seaweed and simmer for 6 minute .
11. Add 2 cups of hot water to the sauce pan and let cook for 5 minutes.
12. Add the egunsi paste, 1 tbsp at a time and cook. Do not stir yet.
13. Stir after 10 minutes, add the spinach and stir, then cover the pot and cook for another 3 minutes.
14. Serve with swallow of choice.

## Beef Stew

### Ingredients

2cups of Beef Seitan( see seitan recipe)

3 tbsp cooking oil

4 large Beefsteak Tomatoes

2 clove Garlic

2 Red Bell Peppers

1 Onion

1 tbsp Fresh Ginger Root

2 vegetable Maggi Cubes

1 Scotch bonnet pepper

1/2 cup vegetable stock

## Direction

In a blender add the washed and halved tomatoes, red peppers, 1 onion, 2 garlic and scotch bonnet pepper. Blend until completely smooth.
In a pot add 1 cup of cooking oil along with 1 chopped onion bring to high heat and cook the onion till translucent.

Pour in one can of tomato paste along with the blended tomato mixture and all the remaining seasonings. Cooked uncovered stirring regularly for 10 minutes to cook the tomatoes. Then add in the vegetable stock and cover the pot cooking on a medium to low heat for an additional 20 minutes. Stirring every so often, you do not want to burn the tomatoes rather just fry them.

Once the oil has come to the top of the pot/tomatoes, add in the beef seitan and allow it to simmer on low heat for 5 minutes. Enjoy!

# Swallows (Fufu)

### Quinoa Swallow

- 2 cups of quinoa flour or blended quinoa
- 1 tsp grounded flax seed
- 1 tsp psyllium husk
- 2 cups of water.

### Direction

- Boil 2 cups of water in a medium sauce pan on medium heat
- In a medium size bowl mix the quinoa flour, flax seed and psyllium husk
- Once the water is boiled mix the flour mix into the water little by little until you get a fufu texture. Pound or stir so there is no lump in the fufu.
- Enjoy with your favourite stew.

# Broccoli Swallow(fufu)

- 1 head of broccoli
- 1 tbsp psyllium husk

**Direction**

- Wash and cut the broccoli in pieces
- Transfer it into a pot over medium heat, fill the pot halfway with water and cook 12 minutes
- Once cooked, transfer it to a bowl and blend it with hand blender.
- Add the psyllium husk and keep blending until you get fufu texture.
- Serve with your favourite stew

## Eggplant Swallow

- 1 medium eggplant
- 1 teaspoon Psyllium Husk
- 1 tsp grounded flax seed

## Direction

1. Wash and chop the eggplant into pieces to make blending easier.
2. Blend with as little water as possible and pour into a muslin bag or sifter to remove excess water
3. When all the water has seeped out, put the eggplant puree into a pot on medium heat, stir
4. When it heats up, check the time and continue stirring for 5 minutes.
5. Add the psyllium husk and flax seed and continue stirring for 2 more minutes or until you get fufu texture
6. Serve with your favourite stew.

## Cauliflower Swallow

### Ingredients

*   1 head Cauliflower or 1.5lbs of Cauliflower Florets
*   1tbsp grounded flax seed
*   2 tbsp psyllium husk

Direction:

1.  Cut one head of cauliflower into florets and wash.
2.  Put in blender and add enough water to blend
3.  Blend on high.
4.  Pour in a cheese cloth or sifter to get rid of excess water.
5.  Put in a pot on medium low heat and stir.
6.  Add your psyllium husk and flax seed and stir some more.
7.  Stir untill the consistency is like a paste.
8.  Serve with your soup of choice.

## Butternut Squash Swallow

### Ingredients

- ½ head butternut squash peeled and deseeded
- 2 tablespoon psyllium husk
- 1 tsp grounded flax seed
- 3 cups of water

### Directions

1. Take the peel and deseeded squash and cut It into pieces
2. Add about 3 cups of water with 1 tbsp salt to cook the squash
3. Cook until tender and soft
4. Use hand blender or regular blender to mash it.
5. Add the psyllium husk and flax seed and mix until you get a fufu texture.
6. Enjoy

## Cabbage Swallow

### Ingredients

- 1 head of cabbage chopped
- 1 cup of water
- 1 tsp flaxseed

### Direction

1. Add the chopped cabbage and water into the blender and blend
2. Once blended sift it remove excess water
3. Pour the dried mixture onto a pot over medium heat and stir
4. Add the flax seed and keep stirring until you get fufu consistency.
5. Enjoy.

**Mushroom Swallow**

**Ingredients**

- 2 packs of white mushroom
- 3 tbsp water
- 1 tbsp psyllium husk

**Directions**

1. Wash and dry the mushrooms
2. Boil the mushroom with 3 tbsp of water until brown
3. Once cooled transfer to a bowl and blend with hand blender
4. Add the psyllium husk and keep stirring until you get a fufu texture.
5. Let it cool and enjoy.

# Coconut Fufu

# Ingredients

- 2 cups of dried coconut flour(you can make your own or buy it)
- 1 tbsp psyllium husk
- 1 tbsp grounded flax seed

## Direction
1. In a medium bowl add coconut flour, flax and psyllium
2. Mix together
3. On the stove bring 2 cups of water to a boil
4. Once the water is boiled add the flour mixture.
5. Stir until you get fufu texture.
6. Serve with your favourite stew

## Bean Sprout

### Ingredients

- 3 cups of bean sprout
- 1 tbsp psyllium husk

### Direction

- Wash the bean sprout
- Pour the bean sprout into a pot and fill halfway with water
- Cook for 12 minutes over medium heat. Once cooked
- Drain the water off
- Blend it to remove any lumps then add the psyllium
- Stir with wooden spoon until you get the fufu consistency
- Serve with favourite stew

# Plaintain Fufu

- 1 unriped plaintain
- ½ cup water

## Direction

1. Take the skin off the plaintain and cut into pieces
2. Add the water and the plaintain pieces into a blender, then blend until smooth
3. Transfer to a pot on the stove over medium heat
4. Keep stirring with wooden spoon until it's cooked. It will have a bright yellow colour and stretchy.
5. Serve with your favourite stew.

I hope you have enjoyed making all the recipes in this cook book. The recipes have blessed my family and I hope it will bless yours too.

I will love to connect with you on social media.

Connect with me on instagram @abbyayoola

If you're looking for Vegan/Vegetarian restaurants that delivers to your area then follow Yummy Dishes @yummydishes18 both on instagram and facebook.www.yummydishes.ca

Tag #africanizingveganfood on your social media with your pictures of the recipes in this cookbook.


Love you all.

Made in the USA
Coppell, TX
03 March 2022

74357507R00074